Math All Around

Measuring at Home

Jennifer Rozines Roy and Gregory Roy

mc **Marshall Cavendish**
Benchmark
New York

How tall is this lamp?

How heavy is this book?

How much is in this glass?

We answer these questions by measuring. When you **measure**, you find out how much there is of something. Measurement is an important part of math.

We can learn about measuring without traveling very far. In fact, you won't have to put your shoes on—we're staying home!

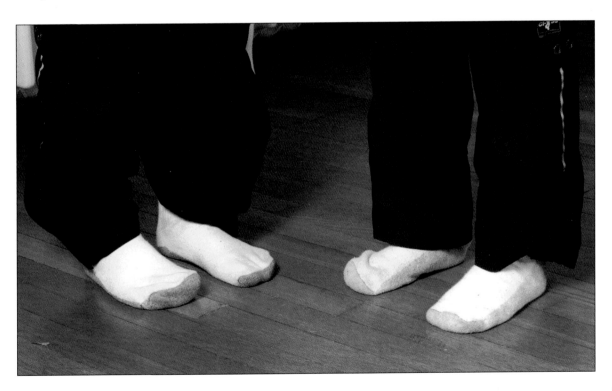

Let's start in the family room. Your family likes to hang out in here. So does your dog.

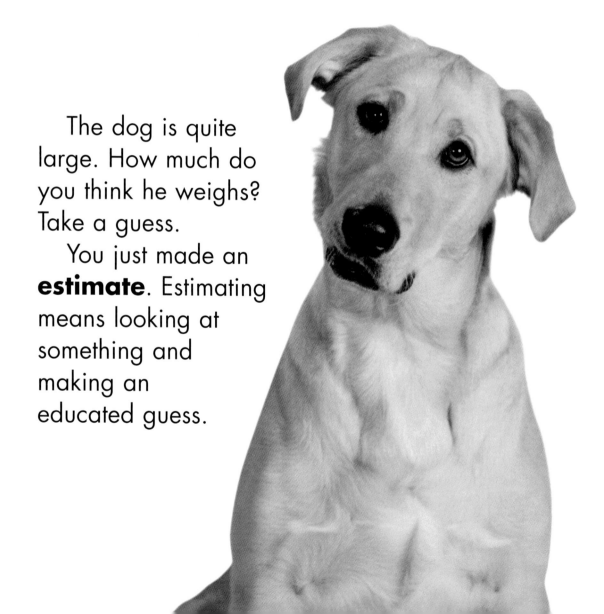

The dog is quite large. How much do you think he weighs? Take a guess.

You just made an **estimate**. Estimating means looking at something and making an educated guess.

The fireplace warms up this room. How warm is it exactly in here?

To find out an exact answer, we don't estimate. That's where measuring comes in!

5

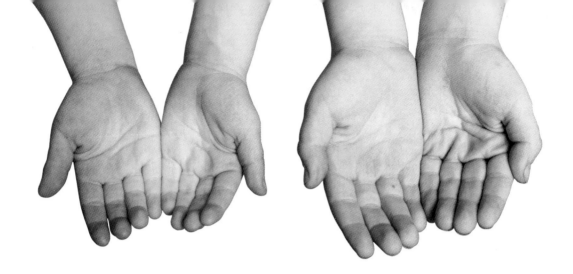

We need special tools to measure. If we used just anything—our hands, our feet, or a bucket—it wouldn't be the same. People's hands and feet are different sizes. And buckets come in all sorts of shapes and sizes.

So to measure exactly, we use a standard measure. A standard measure means that each **unit** is the same when used by different people and in different places.

A pound weighs exactly the same amount in your house as it does in your friend's house, your neighbor's house, or even your teacher's house!

These measuring tools have standard measures.

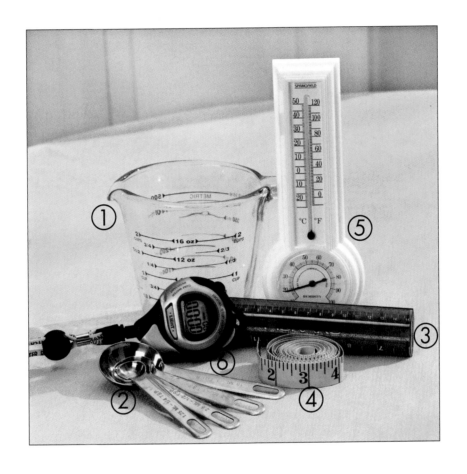

① measuring cup   ④ tape measure
② measuring spoons   ⑤ thermometer
③ ruler   ⑥ stopwatch

Let's do some measuring upstairs. But first let's have some fun getting there!

Using the stopwatch, we can see how long it takes to go from the bottom of the stairs to the top. Hit the stopwatch button and run!

Stop. Click the button again at the top. Eleven seconds!

Opening your bedroom door takes only seconds, too. Seconds are units of time that measure things that happen quickly.

Minutes measure things that take a little longer. Getting dressed takes a few minutes.

Things that take a long time, like a good night's sleep, take hours.

Seconds, minutes, and hours are measured with clocks.

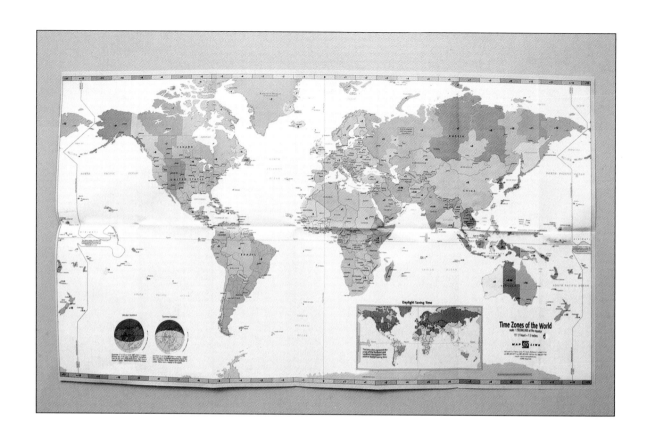

In your bedroom, you have a world map on the wall. All over the world people use seconds, minutes, and hours to measure time!

But not everyone uses the same system as units of measurement for other things.

People in the United States use customary measurements to find out how tall or long or wide things are. Inches, feet, yards, and miles are units of measurement in the **customary system**.

Let's look at our measuring tape. One side shows inches. Inches measure things that aren't too big.

Let's find something that can be measured with inches.

Let's use the measuring tape to find out the height of this stuffed animal.

First, unroll the tape. Put the end of the tape at the eagle's claws. Make sure you have the correct end of the tape. You'll need the end that starts with the number one.

Hold up the tape. The top of the eagle's head reaches the fourteen inch mark. The eagle stands 14 inches tall.

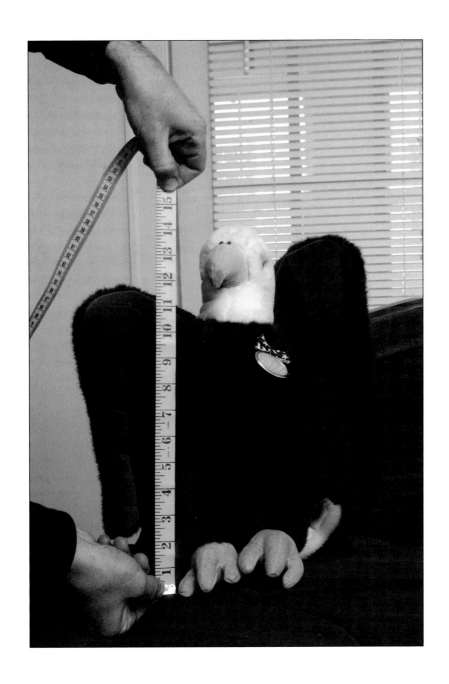

Now flip over the measuring tape. The other side shows units of measurement called centimeters. Centimeters are used in the **metric system**, which is used by most other countries around the world.

Centimeters, meters, and kilometers are units of measurement in the metric system.

Let's measure the eagle again using the metric system.

This eagle is 35.5 centimeters tall. It also is 14 inches tall. It is the same eagle. You just used different systems of measurement.

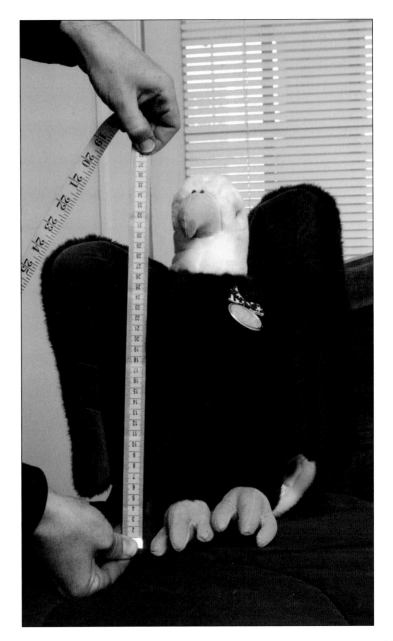

In the bathroom, a scale is on the floor. A scale measures **weight**. Weight is the **force** of **gravity** on something. We weigh things to find out how heavy they are.

The customary units for weight are pound and ounce. The metric units are gram, milligram, and kilogram.

Step on the scale. Wow! You are 66 pounds or 30 kilograms.

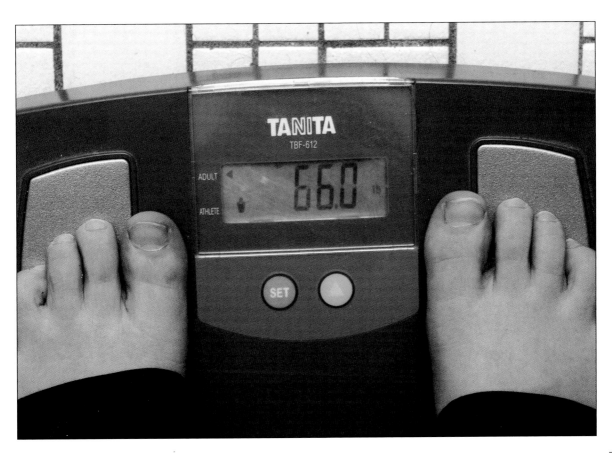

Mom is in the kitchen making cookies.

Here is the recipe:

Chocolate Chip Cookies

1/4 cup brown sugar
1/2 cup butter
1 cup flour
1 teaspoon vanilla
1 six-ounce package
    chocolate chips
1 egg

Cups, teaspoons, and ounces are all units of measurement. If we measure the ingredients correctly, we'll get a tasty treat!

Have a glass of milk with your cookies! Open the refrigerator. A thermometer is inside. A thermometer is a tool for measuring temperature. Temperature is measured in degrees. Degrees tell how warm or cold something is.

The temperature is 40 degrees Fahrenheit. The thermometer also shows the temperature in metric units called degrees Celsius. The thermometer reads 4.4 degrees Celsius. Cool enough to keep food cold!

Grab the jug of milk. The amount of something inside a container is called the **volume**. The milk jug says its volume is one gallon.

This carton of juice is smaller. It is one quart. And here is an even smaller one—a pint of cream.

Gallons, quarts, and pints are units of measurement, too.

Enjoy your milk and cookies!

We've measured our way around the house! In any room you can find things of all different sizes, weights, and volumes.

Measuring is a great way to learn more about the world around us—and the house around us!

How do you measure up?

Glossary

customary system — A method of measurement used mostly in the United States.

estimate — A rough or approximate guess.

force — A push or pull of a thing against something else.

gravity — The attraction of an object to the earth.

measure — To find out the size or amount of something.

metric system — A system of weights and measures in which units go up or down by tens, hundreds, or thousands.

unit — An amount used as a standard of measurement.

volume — The amount of space inside something that has length, width, and height.

weight — The force of gravity on something; how heavy something is.

Read More

Bull, Jane. *Change Your Room*. Dorling Kindersley, 1999.

Hightower, Susan. *Twelve Snails to One Lizard: A Tale of Mischief and Measurement*. Simon & Schuster, 1997.

Web Sites

AAAKnow Math: Measurements
www.aaaknow.com/mea.htm

Funbrain: Measure It!
www.funbrain.com/measure/index.html

Index

Page numbers in **boldface** are illustrations.

About the Authors

Jennifer Rozines Roy is the author of more than twenty books. A former Gifted and Talented teacher, she holds degrees in psychology and elementary education.

Gregory Roy is a civil engineer who has co-authored several books with his wife. The Roys live in upstate New York with their son Adam.

Marshall Cavendish Benchmark
99 White Plains Road
Tarrytown, New York 10591-9001
www.marshallcavendish.us

Library of Congress Cataloging-in-Publication Data

Roy, Jennifer Rozines, 1967–
Measuring at home / by Jennifer Rozines Roy and Gregory Roy.
p. cm. — (Math all around)
Summary: "Introduces the concept of measuring to record height, weight, volume, time, and temperature, including the use of measuring
tools. Stimulates critical thinking and provides students with an understanding of math in the real world"—Provided by publisher.
Includes index.
ISBN-13: 978-0-7614-2263-1
ISBN-10: 0-7614-2263-3
1. Mensuration—Juvenile literature. 2. Measuring instruments—Juvenile literature. I. Roy, Gregory. II. Title. III. Series.
QA465.R698 2006
516'.15—dc22
2006008175

Photo Research by Anne Burns Images

Cover Photo by *Woodfin Camp*/Catherine Karnow

The photographs in this book are used with permission and through the courtesy of:
Jay Mallin: pp. 1, 2C, 3, 6, 7, 8, 9, 10, 12, 13, 15, 16, 17, 18, 19, 23, 24(all). *Corbis*: p. 2T C. Schmidt/zefa;
p. 25 William Deering/Picture Arts. *Index Stock*: p. 2B Robert & Laura Schimitschek. *Superstock*: p. 4 Purestock; p. 5 Steven S. Miric;
p. 11L&R Comstock; p. 20 Superstock; p. 21T Food Collecton; p. 21C Image Source; p. 21B Comstock; p. 26 Blend Images.

Series design by Virginia Pope

Printed in Malaysia
1 3 5 6 4 2